GW01045605

191

Herbert Galloway Stewart's Diary of the Russian Revolution

First Edition 2016

Published by

The Stewart Museum,

Burnby Hall Gardens and Museum,

Pocklington, YO42 2QF

ISBN 978-0-9928328-3-4

A Witness To Revolution

"Much shooting and many disturbances in the streets. Some regiments joined the revolutionaries. Officers walking were disarmed. Prisons opened. Police stations attacked. Prison close to Palace attacked by large crowds – much shooting all round…"

So begins the entry for Monday 12th March 1917 in a small blue diary displayed in the Stewart Museum at Burnby Hall Gardens in Pocklington, East Yorkshire.

Plain in design, with its front cover embossed with the words "Diary" and "1917" in gold leaf, this little book has a fascinating story to tell.

In March 1917, its owner, Herbert Galloway Stewart, began writing a short series of diary entries which provide an eye-witness account of the early days of the Russian Revolution in Petrograd (St Petersburg), told from the unique perspective of an Englishman in the employment of the Romanov family.

At first-hand, he saw how order broke down, how attempts were made to restore it, and the ultimate fall of the Romanov dynasty which had ruled the country for over three hundred years.

This Stewart Museum booklet marks the centenary of the diary being written.

Herbert Stewart was the son of a Huntingdonshire clergyman. From 1908 to 1917 he was employed as English tutor to the children of the Grand Duke Alexander Michailovitch, brother-in-law of Tsar Nicholas II.

Petrograd in 1915 – Photograph by Herbert Stewart
(National Media Museum)

Living as part of their household at 106, Moika in Petrograd, he was ideally placed to record events as they unfolded, and how they impacted upon one of the highest ranking aristocratic families in Imperial Russia.

The Russia that Herbert lived and worked in was a troubled country. Unrest caused by rapid industrialisation; vast inequalities in wealth between rich and poor, in both the cities and the countryside; political upheaval following the introduction of a constitutional-style monarchy from 1905; increased public concerns about the influence of Rasputin on the Tsar and his wife; all of these factors contributed to an increasingly deteriorating situation.

But it was the First World War which proved to be the catalyst that brought everything crashing down. Russian defeats, heavy losses, and an army ill-prepared to fight the war machine of Kaiser Wilhelm II's Germany engendered further discontent at home.

Everything came to a head in February 1917 (Russian calendar) when riots and strikes took place in Petrograd, troops mutinied, and crowds singing the Marseillaise thronged the streets of the city.

Order broke down and, in an attempt to restore order to a highly volatile situation, a Provisional Government was established. Everything was on a knife-edge.

Revolution had come, the old regime was being swept away, and foreign nationals in Petrograd, including Herbert Stewart, became witnesses to the cataclysmic events which were taking place around them.

Herbert Stewart
(Stewart Museum)

Herbert Stewart's Diary

Herbert Stewart's diary has been transcribed verbatim using his punctuation, grammatical errors and spellings. The entries combine details of his daily life set alongside dramatic accounts of the events taking place on the streets of Petrograd.

Thursday, March 8 – *"Feb 23. 106 Moika Petrograd. Factories left off working. Many people in the streets. Mostly quiet. I received permission to send home £500."*

Friday, March 9 – *"Went to Credit Lyonnais withdrew R7250 and sent £500 to Coutts through Volga Kama Bank. Many people walking in the streets, crowds in some places, some demanding bread – frequent collisions with police. Cossacks riding about to disperse people. Disturbances on Nevsky and Litanie. I called at British Embassy and saw Lindley [1] after tea also visited Moldehuke – walked everywhere as there were no trams. Palace guarded."*

Saturday, March 10 – *"Crowds about the streets again with occasional disturbances chiefly on Nevsky, Litanie and Vasilievsky Ostrof but nothing very alarming. No trams. Many people wearing red. Visited the Pockvesniffs in the evening and remained late playing Bridge. Palace guarded."*

Sunday, March 11 – *"Many people about. General talk of revolution but nothing serious done. Palace guarded. The Grand Duke Michael Alexandrovitch [2] came in the afternoon* *and gave me leave to fish his water at Zaretchie this year and take a friend. No trams."*

Monday, March 12 - *"Much shooting and many disturbances in the streets. Some regiments joined the revolutionaries. Officers walking were disarmed. Prisons opened. Police stations attacked. Prison close to Palace attacked by large crowds – much shooting all round. Palace guarded till evening when guard was removed. I dined with de Châtelain. Much uncertainty about everything but eventually it was announced that Duma was setting up provisional government, and that the Emperor had been asked to come. Protopopoff (3) and other disliked ministers dismissed. No trams."*

Tuesday, March 13 – *"Firing continued nearly all last night and began again early in the morning. I went out into the Moika – many people about especially round the Prison which was set on fire later in the day. Frederick's (Count) (4) house on Post Office Street burnt. Police headquarters in Fontanka also burnt. I walked in the garden after lunch – not pleasant owing to continual rifle and machine gun shooting. Provisional Govmt made provision for patrolling streets, took allegiance of several regiments. Emperor expected tomorrow. Astoria hotel (5) entered by crowd and cleaned out of provisions. Several police stations destroyed and many people arrested and taken to Duma. Our gates open all day – no guards but no unpleasantness. No trams."*

Wednesday, March 14 – *"Less disturbed than the last two days but still some shooting in places. Emperor expected in morning but did not arrive. Various explanations given – some saying prevented by socialistic workmen – it was rumoured that after reaching Luban he had returned towards Moscow. I walked round without molestation in afternoon and saw Frederick's house and the Prison, both still burning. Many people and soldiers about mostly wearing red. Many motors with armed soldiers and nurses patrolling streets, crowds in some places otherwise more or less orderly. No trams. Called at the Pockvesniffs in afternoon. Three of our motors requisitioned by Government."*

Thursday, March 15 - *"Streets more or less quiet – constantly patrolled by motors. Emperor said to be at Pskoff. It is rumoured that the workmen want Republic while Provisional Govmt want Constitutional Govmt Soldiers wishes at present unknown but it is said there is general feeling against present Emperor. Govmt receiving allegiance of officers and others. Stated in paper that Great Britain and France prepared to support general wishes of Russian people. I visited Messrs Lindley, Bray, Hubbard and the Pockvesniffs. Grand Duke Nicholas Michailovitch (6) arrived here. Soldiers took all guns and ammunition from the palace including sporting weapons. Not altogether unlikely that they were simple thieves as they stole boots and other things as well. Rumours about that Dvinsk and Riga were taken, probably untrue. Later it turned out to be untrue. Some shops open. Very few istvostchiks."*

Friday, March 16 – *"Took letters to the Embassy and afterwards called at Marshalls. They had unpleasant times with several visits from soldiers. Count Stackelburg taken from next house to them on Wednesday and killed on Quay. The Emperor abdicated and left throne to his brother who refused to accept, leaving decision to the Russian people.*

Petrograd in 1915 - Photograph by Herbert Stewart
(National Media Museum)

Many people in streets but more order and no shooting. Met General Poole at Marshalls, he had been in Astoria but moved to Europe when the hotel was wrecked by insurgents. Heard that Oliver Locker – Lampson (7) was at Astoria, called, found him out and left message promising to call again tomorrow. Provisional Government appointed new ministers acceptable to Constitutionalists and Republicans. No work and no trams at present. Reported that all servants at Tsarskoe Selo deserted but that no serious disturbance arose and that now all is quiet and palace guarded. Called at Pockvesniffs and exchanged news. met the son for the first time. he had arrived the night before. Heavy depression at 106 and no wonder."

Saturday, March 17 – *"Found Oliver in the morning at Marsden's and asked him to tea today. He could not come being too busy over English post. Streets very full but all quiet. Most shops open, bought cigarettes. Anitchkoff Palace much marked with bullets. Many recruits coming in. A few istvostchiks and private sleighs to be seen but no trams. Called at Pockvesniffs and took letters to Embassy, where they have a guard from the Page Corps. Red flag over winter Palace and all imperial arms covered with Red. Tram wires over new bridge broken down. Still uncertainty about eventual form of government but things for the moment look better. Stated that general work will begin only on Tuesday. Motor cars still requisitioned. Oliver's car the only one I know of that is available for himself and his friends. He very kindly offered me the use of it when it is free. Reported today that Tsarevitch was dead of course untrue. Yesterday's report that German Emperor dead and Crown Prince wounded was contradicted. Sabounoffs came in the evening. Gave Princess Dolgorouky some photos in afternoon. Wrote Wishaw. Isobel."*

Sunday March 18 – *"I went to church this morning, expecting to join in hymn 'O God our help in ages past' and was not disappointed. In afternoon took letter to Princess Obolensky 57 Sergievskaia. Oliver lent me motor to go there. I walked back. Called also at Countess Orloff. 27. she was out. Heard that serious trouble at Helsingfoss when fleet had mutinied and killed many officers. Many people in streets and processions headed by red flags going to Duma with various demands. One asking for division of crown lands. Saw no disturbances. More istvostchiks and sleighs about today. Prayer in church for governing powers of Russia. Heard that The Empress Marie had gone to her son. Our palace is guarded by sailors now, night and day".*

Key:

1. Probably Sir Francis Oswald Lindley, Counsellor of the British Embassy in Petrograd.
2. Younger brother of Tsar Nicholas II.
3. Minister of the Interior under Nicholas II.
4. Minister of the Imperial Court.
5. Many members of the British Intelligence Mission were billeted here.
6. Brother of Grand Duke Alexander Michailovitch.
7. Commander Oliver Locker Lampson, Royal Naval Armoured Car Division.

Notes:

As it is a Western-style English diary, the dates given are thirteen days in advance of the Gregorian calendar in use in Russia in 1917. So, for example, the 8th of March (Western calendar) was the 23rd February (Russian calendar).

Unanswered Questions

The diary raises some interesting questions:

What was Herbert's connection with Commander Oliver Locker Lampson, who features three times in the diary?

He was a Royal Naval Armoured Car Division officer who became closely involved in Russian politics over this period and later claimed to have had a secret plan to rescue Tsar Nicholas II following his abdication.

In her book *Ekaterinburg*, Helen Rappaport writes:

"Lampson had got to know the Tsar at HQ at Mogilev, and after Nicholas' confinement at Tsarskoe Selo had deemed the opportunities for rescue very easy. Bribing the already careless guards with cigarettes, vodka and British bully beef, Lampson had planned that one of the Tsar's servants would don a false beard and cloak and take his place, Nicholas meanwhile disguising himself in a British khaki uniform that Lampson had smuggled in, shaving off his beard and walking out of the palace in front of the drunken guards. From there a field ambulance would take him to a military train and north to Archangel and a British ship to the UK. The same ploy, however, could not of course be used with Alexandra and the children; the Tsar had refused point blank to be rescued unless they could be saved too, proving himself, in Lampson's eyes, 'a true king and a true man'…"

Nicholas II – Photograph by Herbert Stewart
(National Media Museum)

Given his apparent friendship with Locker Lampson, did Herbert know anything of this bizarre escape plan?

It is hard to imagine the uncertainty and fear that must have been felt by Herbert and those like him who found themselves in Petrograd as the Russian Revolution began.

Executions on the streets, marauding gangs of revolutionaries, and the breakdown of law and order would have been a terrifying and potentially life-threatening experience for foreign nationals living there, particularly those with connections to the old regime.

Yet, following the departure of his employers to the Crimea, Herbert remained in the city for several months.

He knew a British officer planning to rescue the Tsar; he frequented the Astoria Hotel, where the British Intelligence Mission was billeted; he stayed on in Petrograd when he could surely have returned home; and whilst there is no evidence to suggest that he was involved in any political intrigue himself, his movements and connections over this period do remain curious and interesting.

And then we have the diary:

Why, with the exception of the eleven entries referred to, is the rest of this amazing document left completely empty?

One hundred years on, I guess we'll never know for certain.

Herbert Stewart's Diary
(Stewart Museum)

Acknowledgements

My thanks to the following in the preparation of this booklet:

- The Stewart Museum at Burnby Hall Gardens, Pocklington.
- The National Media Museum, Bradford for allowing me to use Herbert Stewart's photographs on pages 3, 9 and 13 of this booklet.
- Margaret Revell, niece of Herbert Stewart, for providing additional archive materials.
- Helen Rappaport for allowing me to quote from page 120 of her book *Ekaterinburg*.
- Museums Development Yorkshire for providing funding assistance.

Sources

- Herbert Stewart's Diary – Stewart Museum.
- The Stewart Museum Archive.
- *Mr Stewart and the Romanovs* – Peter Rogers 2014.

Cover Picture: A silhouette of Herbert Stewart in 1919 (Margaret Revell).